Comparing
People From
the Past

Pieter Bruegel the Elder
and L.S. Lowry

Nick Hunter

raintree

a Capstone company — publishers for children

Raintree is an imprint of Capstone Global Library Limited, a company incorporated in England and Wales having its registered office at 7 Pilgrim Street, London EC4V 6LB – Registered company number: 6695582

www.raintreepublishers.co.uk
myorders@raintreepublishers.co.uk

Edited by Linda Staniford
Designed by Richard Parker
Original illustrations © Capstone Global Library Ltd 2015
Picture research by Tracy Cummins
Production by Victoria Fitzgerald
Originated by Capstone Global Library Ltd
Printed and bound in China b Leo Paper Products

ISBN 978 1 406 29640 2
19 18 17 16 15
10 9 8 7 6 5 4 3 2 1

British Library Cataloguing in Publication Data
A full catalogue record for this book is available from the British Library.

Acknowledgements
We would like to thank the following for permission to reproduce photographs: Alamy: Brian Stark, 19, The Keasbury-Gordon Photograph Archive, 23; Bridgeman Images: Adolphe Valette/Manchester Art Gallery UK, 15, Hendrick van Cleve, 9, © The Estate of L.S. Lowry. All Rights Reserved, DACS/ARS 2014, 22, The Stapleton Collection, 8; Capstone Press: 16; Getty Images: Archive Photos, Cover, Art Media/Print Collector, 20, Hulton Archive, 28, Paul Popper/Popperfoto, 25, Three Lions, 14, Tony Evans, 6, 7, 10, 29, Cover; Newscom: Glyn Satterley NI Syndication, 18; Oxford Designers and Illustrators: 11, 12; Shutterstock: Azuzl, Design Element, Paul Reid, 27, vierra, Design Element; SuperStock: Fine Art Images, 24; Wikimedia: Google Art Project, 4, 5, 13, 17, 21, 26.

Contents

Some words are shown in bold, **like this.** You can find out what they mean by looking in the glossary.

Who was Pieter Bruegel the Elder?

Pieter Bruegel the Elder lived almost 500 years ago. He was a well-known artist during his lifetime. Bruegel's fame has grown because his paintings tell us so much about the people and times he lived in.

We are not sure what Bruegel looked like. He may have painted himself in this **portrait**.

When Bruegel was alive there were no photographs or TV pictures to show how ordinary people looked and dressed. Not many artists painted pictures of ordinary life like Bruegel did.

Who was L.S. Lowry?

Laurence Stephen (L.S.) Lowry is one of the most famous English artists. He started to paint just over 100 years ago. Lowry only became well known after he had been painting for many years.

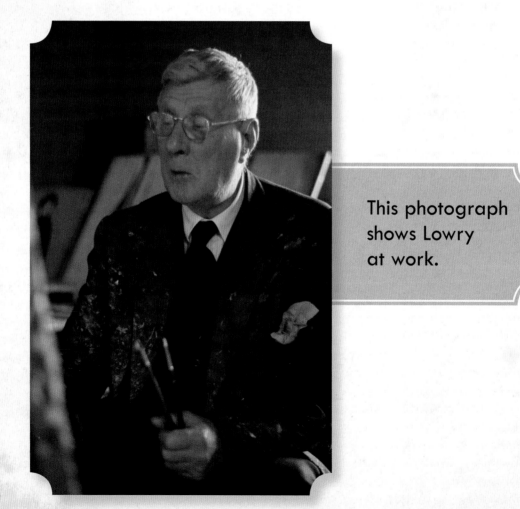

This photograph shows Lowry at work.

Lowry's paintings show how people lived and worked in his **community**. Lowry lived in Northwest England. He painted the people and scenes he saw around him.

Early life

Bruegel was born in the Netherlands around 1525. He probably learned how to paint as an **apprentice** to Pieter Coecke van Aelst in Brussels. Van Aelst was a well-known artist who had worked at the royal **court**.

Artists learned their trade by working in the studio of a more experienced painter.

This picture shows what Rome looked like in Bruegel's time.

The centre of the art world was Italy.
Many young artists travelled there
to learn from the world's best artists.
Bruegel visited Italy as a young man.
He spent time in the ancient city of Rome.

Lowry was born on 1 November 1887 in Manchester, England. He had no brothers or sisters. When Lowry was still a child, his family moved to the nearby **industrial** town of Pendlebury.

Lowry took inspiration from the factories and mills he saw in Pendlebury.

This map shows Manchester, in Northwest England, where Lowry lived and worked.

Greater Manchester

Pendlebury

Salford

Manchester

Lowry always loved drawing. He said he began to paint when he was 15 years old. Lowry learned about other great artists at Manchester **College** of Art and Salford Royal Technical College.

Where and when did they live?

Bruegel lived and worked in the cities of Antwerp and Brussels, which are now in Belgium. These were two of the biggest and busiest cities in Europe. Many artists lived and worked there.

This map shows the Netherlands, the country where Bruegel lived and worked.

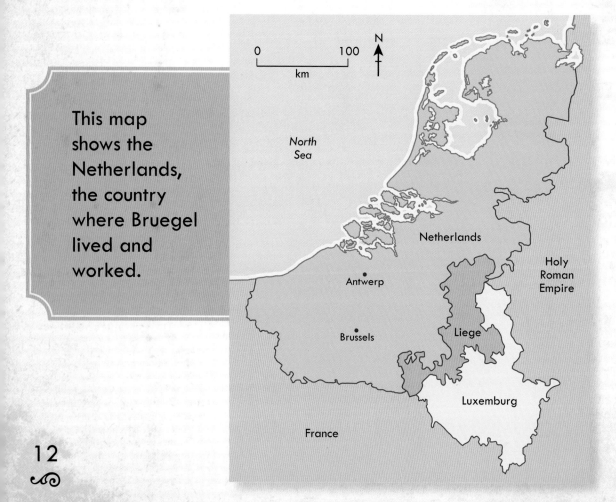

Bruegel lived during a time of great change called the **Renaissance.** The first printed books were helping to spread new ideas and knowledge across the world. Artists were learning new ways of painting.

Lowry spent almost his whole life living and working around Manchester. He worked as a **rent collector.** He kept this job a secret, because he wanted people to think he worked as an artist all the time.

Lowry's job helped him to explore the streets around Manchester.

This picture of foggy Manchester was painted by Adolphe Valette, one of Lowry's teachers.

When Lowry started painting, people could already see the world in photos and even movies. This is why artists tried to show the world differently. Paintings can show the feelings of the characters and the feelings of the artist.

What did they do?

Bruegel worked as a painter and **engraver** in a workshop in Antwerp. His early engravings followed the style of popular artists of the time, but he soon created his own style of painting.

This picture shows Bruegel at work in his studio.

Artists like Bruegel needed rich supporters, like this merchant, to buy their paintings.

In 1563, Bruegel moved to Brussels. He started to create the paintings that would make him famous. His paintings showed ordinary people in scenes where they are working or enjoying themselves.

Lowry painted in his spare time and late at night. He painted scenes from his local area, such as factories and football matches. Lowry also painted **portraits** of people, including himself.

Local scenery like this inspired Lowry.

Lowry lived in this house in Pendlebury for most of his life.

For most of his life, Lowry's work was not well known. Later in life, his paintings of ordinary people and their working lives became famous.

What's so special about their paintings?

Pieter Bruegel was called "**Peasant** Bruegel" because his paintings showed scenes from peasant life. Other artists painted scenes from the Bible, or **portraits** of rich and important people.

Italian artist Titian painted this picture about the same time that Bruegel was working.

This painting shows children's toys and the games they played almost 500 years ago.

Bruegel's paintings show us how ordinary people dressed, what they ate and even the games they played. They can help us to understand how people lived in Bruegel's time.

Lowry painted the **mills**, factories and people he saw around him. Most artists in his time did not try to show how ordinary people lived. Today, many people still love Lowry's clear but detailed pictures.

Lowry painted *At the Mill Gate* in 1945.

This photo shows Manchester in the 1930s. What similarities and differences can you spot between this picture and Lowry's paintings?

Lowry was painting less than 100 years ago, but he showed a changing world. The factories and **communities** he painted disappeared during his life. Lowry's paintings help us to remember them.

Family life

Bruegel married Mayken Coecke van Aelst in 1563. Mayken was the daughter of Bruegel's teacher. The couple had two sons who both became artists. The older son is known as Pieter Bruegel the Younger. Bruegel died in 1569, when he was around 45 years old.

Bruegel died when his sons were very young. They were taught to paint by their grandmother.

PETRVS BREVGEL
ANTVERPIÆ PICTOR RVRALIVM ACTIONVM.

In his later years, Lowry became a famous artist.

Lowry lived with his mother until she died in 1939. In 1948, he moved to the countryside. His later paintings included **portraits** and pictures of the sea. He died in 1976, aged 88.

Remembering Bruegel and Lowry

We do not know much about Bruegel's life apart from what we can learn from his paintings. The only account of his life was written after he died. Many of his paintings were lost.

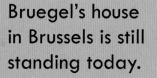

Bruegel's house in Brussels is still standing today.

The Lowry Centre in Salford is a concert hall and art gallery.

Lowry created more than 10,000 paintings and drawings. They can be seen in many art galleries. A large collection of Lowry's work is displayed in a special gallery in Salford, near where he lived and painted.

Comparing Bruegel

Pieter Bruegel the Elder

| Born | Around 1525 |

| Died | 1569 |

Career

Professional artist who became master of a painters' **guild** in Antwerp in 1551

Family life

Married with two children, who both went on to be artists

Fascinating fact

Bruegel would sometimes dress in the clothes of a **peasant** so he could blend in with ordinary people and get ideas for his paintings.

Famous people living at the same time

Michelangelo (artist, 1475–1564)
Elizabeth I (Queen of England, 1533–1603)
Nicolaus Copernicus (astronomer who proved that Earth orbits the Sun, 1473–1543)

1400   1500   **PIETER BRUEGEL**   1600   1700

and Lowry

L.S. Lowry

Born	1887
Died	1976

Career

Worked as **rent collector** in Manchester before retiring in 1952; painted in the evenings and at weekends

Family life

Lived with his mother until her death; never married

Fascinating fact

Although cars became hugely popular in Lowry's lifetime, he never included cars in his pictures.

Famous people living at the same time

Sir Winston Churchill (British Prime Minister, 1874–1965)
John Logie Baird (inventor of television, 1888–1946)
Barbara Hepworth (British sculptor, 1903–1975)

L.S. LOWRY

1800   1900   2000

Glossary

apprentice person who learns how to do something by working with more experienced people

college place where people go to study after finishing school

community group of people who live in a town or a particular place

court place where a king or queen lives to rule a country

engraver person who creates designs or pictures that can be printed on a printing press

guild organization or society of workers or craftspeople

industrial place with lots of factories and other similar buildings

mill type of factory, particularly one that is used to make textiles

peasant name used in the past for poor farmers or labourers and their families

portrait picture of a person

Renaissance period which began around 1400, when new ideas in art, politics and science spread around the world

rent collector someone who works collecting rent money

Find out more

Books

Pieter Bruegel the Elder (History Heroes), Damian Harvey and Yulyia Somina (Franklin Watts, 2014)

The Art Book for Children (Phaidon, 2005)

The Little Lowry, Catherine De Duve (Happy Museum, 2013)

The Story of Painting, Abigail Wheatley (Usborne, 2013)

Websites

www.bbc.co.uk/learningzone/clips/the-inspiration-behind-l-s-lowrys-work/4125.html

There is a short film from the BBC about Lowry's art on this website.

www.pieter-bruegel-the-elder.org

This website includes information about Bruegel's life and many of his paintings.

www.thelowry.com/ls-lowry/microsite/home

Here you can find everything you need to know about Lowry's life.

Index